T0132387

The Long Journey Home

Vivian Salama

Archway Publishing books may be ordered through booksellers or by contacting:

Archway Publishing
1663 Liberty Drive
Bloomington, IN 47403
www.archwaypublishing.com
1 (888) 242-5904

ISBN: 978-1-4808-7431-2 (sc)
ISBN: 978-1-4808-7432-9 (hc)
ISBN: 978-1-4808-7430-5 (e)

Print information available on the last page.

Archway Publishing rev. date: 3/28/2019

For my parents.

Every day, Hassan and his sister, Lina, walked to the school five blocks from their home in Syria. Hassan studied math, science, history, and other subjects. But Hassan's favorite thing to do was play soccer with his friends.

We journey towards a home not of our flesh.
Its chestnut trees are not of our bones.
Its rocks are not like goats in the mountain hymn.
The pebbles' eyes are not lilies.
We journey towards a home that does not halo our heads with a special sun.
Mythical women applaud us. A sea for us, a sea against us.
When water and wheat are not at hand, eat our love and drink our tears...

--Mahmoud Darwish

Hassan burst into his home and ran toward his mother, shouting, "We won! We won!"

"That's great, Hassan," his mom said, giving him a big hug.

"And guess who scored the winning goal ... meeee," he shouted, throwing his hands up in the air.

"My sweetheart," she said. "I'll make your favorite food for dinner. Meatballs!"

While doing his homework after dinner, his parents sat in the next room watching the news. Hassan couldn't help but overhear what the woman on the news said.

"Daddy, what's a protest?" Hassan asked.

"The people are gathered in the streets because they are demanding change," Hassan's father said.

"Change what?" Hassan asked.

His dad pulled little Hassan onto his lap. "These people want more rights, Hassan. They want to be able to speak their minds without the police sending them to jail. They are dreaming of freedom and respect. Some countries have these rights, but here in Syria, we've never known what it means to be free."

Summer arrived. It was Hassan's favorite season because he could play soccer all day long. Every day after breakfast, he sprinted to the field near his apartment building. His closest friends were always there.

There was Omar, who was a grade above Hassan in school. His long legs helped him outrun all the other boys on the soccer field.

Ahmed lived in Hassan's apartment building. Sometimes when the other boys couldn't make it to the field, Hassan and Ahmed met outside their building to kick the ball around for fun.

Mohammed, Ahmed's older brother, was one of the smartest students at school. He always brought his books to the field and read in between games.

Then there was Samir, Hassan's best friend. Samir always told the funniest jokes and made Hassan laugh until his stomach hurt.

When the school year started again, Hassan headed to the soccer field almost every evening. But as the year went on, he noticed fewer and fewer boys were coming out to play.

Then one day Omar disappeared.

"Where's Omar?" Hassan shouted, worried they'd lose the game without his quick feet.

"I heard his family left Syria," answered Mohammed. "His brother was one of the protesters, so his family got worried that the police would be upset with them. So they left."

"On vacation?" Hassan asked.

"I don't think so. I heard they moved to Germany. They speak a different language there," Mohammed said.

Hassan was so confused. *How could Omar just leave without saying goodbye? Why would they go away forever? How can Omar live in a place where they speak a different language?*

He came into his apartment that night and wasted no time: "Dad, where's Germany?"

But his dad and mom didn't respond. They were glued to the TV. The news, again! Hassan always found the news so boring, and these days, his parents watched it all the time. He never had the TV for himself to watch *Transformers*, his favorite show.

One day, there was a knock at Hassan's front door. It was Samir, Hassan's best friend.

"I've come to say goodbye," Samir said. Samir explained that his family had to leave the country. His parents said it wasn't safe for them anymore. He said bad people in the streets wanted to cause trouble. His parents were worried, and they decided to leave. Hassan could barely say two words before Samir hugged him and ran home.

Hassan closed the door slowly. He couldn't believe this was happening. *Why would bad people want to make trouble for Samir or his family?* he wondered.

Samir didn't say where his family was going. Hassan figured it was that Germany place. He really hated Germany, wherever it was!

His best friend was gone; his soccer buddies too. He went outside and quietly kicked his soccer ball around for hours until his mom called him inside for dinner.

A few weeks later, Hassan came home from school and was surprised to find his father already back from work.

"Hassan, here is a small bag," his father said, handing him a backpack. "I need you to pack quickly. Take only three pieces of clothing. Only the most important things you can't live without. Let's go. We have to move quickly."

Hassan was scared. He didn't understand where they were going or what was happening. But he could tell his parents were really worried.

He could hear Lina crying in the next room. And his mother was praying aloud, asking God to protect them.

He was angry but did as his parents told him and packed his tiny bag with one pair of jeans and three shirts.

As the family walked out the front door, small bags in hand, Hassan shouted: "Wait!" He dropped his bag and ran back to his bedroom. He nearly forgot the most important thing: his soccer ball.

They turned off the lights. His father took one last look through the house as the family waited by the door. It was time to go.

After two long bus rides, everyone got off and lined up near an area with fences. Men in uniform checked people's papers.

As his family got closer, Hassan noticed the men in uniform were speaking a different language. He thought, *This must be Germany! I'll get to see Samir and Omar!"*

He started to get excited. And then he overheard people behind him say that they were entering a country called Turkey. "Turkey?" he thought, feeling disappointed. He remembered studying about Turkey in school and knew it was a country right next to Syria.

After hours of standing in line, they eventually passed the fenced-off area and arrived at a place with tents as far as the eye could see. It looked like a big camping trip. Every family was given a tent, including Hassan's.

They spent the night there. There were mattresses on the floor for them to sleep on. Hassan was very tired and fell asleep right away.

Hassan's father woke him early the next morning. "Son, it's time to go." Hassan rubbed his eyes and looked around the tiny tent. He followed his father without saying a word. The whole family squeezed on to another bus packed with people. Some people had really big bags, while others, like Hassan, had small ones.

Hassan's father said they would be taking a boat next. Hassan was excited. The last time he was on a boat was during a family trip to the city of Latakia two years earlier. But when they got there, he realized it wasn't exactly a boat like the one he'd been on before. This one was a raft. Many people from the bus piled onto the raft with Hassan and his family. It was so crowded that people had to leave their big suitcases behind.

Hassan hoped it would be a quick trip.

The water was rough, and the boat rocked back and forth for hours. Lina was seasick. Hassan was scared. He tried to be brave and hold back his tears, but it was hard. Even some of the grown-ups cried, including Hassan's mother. She kept squeezing Hassan and crying, and praying to God to protect them. Hassan put the soccer ball on his lap and wrapped his arms around it, wishing he were back home in Syria.

The boat continued to rock back and forth. Hassan put his head on the ball and drifted off to sleep.

Hassan woke up to the feeling of a man wrapping a blanket around him and pulling him out of the boat. They made it to land!

When he got ashore, he looked around in a panic. "My ball!" He kicked and screamed. "It's on the boat!"

But no one understood what he was saying because they all spoke different languages. Hassan shouted again and again, until finally, he broke down and cried.

Suddenly, an older man walked up to Hassan. He had the ball! But Hassan didn't understand what he was saying.

"Give me my ball," Hassan demanded. The man didn't answer. "Give me the ball," he shouted, his emotions turning to anger.

The man smiled, put the ball on the ground, and kicked it toward Hassan.

Hassan put his foot on it, never wanting to be separated from his favorite ball again. But the man waved at him to kick it back. He wanted to play.

At first, Hassan hesitated. But then he nervously kicked it
back. Three kids came running over. Hassan kicked the ball to
them as well. They ran up and down the beach where the boat
washed up, laughing and kicking the ball around.

Hassan didn't understand what any of them were saying, but it
didn't matter. He was making friends and playing soccer.

It felt just like home.

Hassan and his family spent a couple of days on that beach, sleeping in one of those tents again. After a few days, Hassan's father said they needed to rush to catch a train.

A train! Hassan had never been on a train. They had to travel in a bus all night long to get to the train station.

Early the next morning, it was time to board. The train was even more wonderful than Hassan had imagined. There were at least twelve train cars attached to each other. Each one had windows and a door in the front and back. The train was a shiny silver color. and smoke came out of a pipe on the front car.

And the best part? Hassan overheard his parents say there was even a restaurant on the train.

The second they boarded the train, Hassan shouted, "I get the window seat," trying to beat his sister to it.

Just before the train pulled out of the station, a loud whistle blew, just like the trains do on TV. It was Hassan's favorite part of the trip.

And off they went.

Many, many hours passed.

Hassan threw his ball up in the air and caught it.

He bounced it off the walls of the train.

He rolled it around under his feet.

A few times he lightly kicked it up and down the aisles of the train just to fight off his boredom. But his mother said that wasn't polite and made him stop.

Hassan and his family spent a day and a night and a day on the train until they arrived at their next stop.

"Where are we, Dad?" he asked sleepily.

"This is a country called Austria, Hassan."

Hassan had never heard of this place, but he saw lots of pretty buildings as they rolled into the train station. But as he got out, he quickly decided he didn't like Austria.

There were lots of people gathered at the train station holding signs with writing couldn't read. At first he thought they we welcoming them to their city. But they d seem happy to see them. They seemed a

Hassan overheard his father say the p were protesters. "Are they like the protes who were in Syria, Dad?" Hassan asked.

"In a way," his father said. "But these are protesting against us. They think we here to take their jobs and cause trouble their country. So they don't want us here

"But we can't go home," Hassan said. "Bad people in Syria are making trouble everyone."

"Yes, Hassan," his father replied. "But people are confusing us with the bad pe

There were lots of people gathered at the train station holding signs with writing Hassan couldn't read. At first he thought they were welcoming them to their city. But they didn't seem happy to see them. They seemed angry.

Hassan overheard his father say the people were protesters. "Are they like the protesters who were in Syria, Dad?" Hassan asked.

"In a way," his father said. "But these people are protesting against us. They think we are here to take their jobs and cause trouble in their country. So they don't want us here."

"But we can't go home," Hassan said. "Bad people in Syria are making trouble for everyone."

"Yes, Hassan," his father replied. "But these people are confusing us with the bad people."

Hassan was speechless. His family wasn't bad! They love each other. They love all the people they meet. He thought: *My father is a gentle man. My mother gives the best hugs. And even though I fight with Lina sometimes, she's a great big sister.*

Hassan's father told them to hurry up so they could avoid any trouble. As they left the train station, Hassan caught a glimpse of one sign that he could read. It said, "We don't want you here!"

Hassan's father made plans for them to stay in a single-room apartment with Uncle Mazen and Auntie Mona, who moved from Syria to Austria about four months earlier. Hassan didn't like staying at Uncle Mazen and Auntie Mona's new house. It was small—too small for six people. He was also bored and lonely.

He tried to get some boys in the neighborhood to play soccer with him. He even brought his favorite ball. But they never took him up on it. They just ignored him. Some even pointed at him and laughed.

Hassan often asked his father how long they would be staying at Uncle Mazen and Auntie Mona's house. "God willing, not long," his father always replied.

Eight months passed. There was no news. No school. And no new friends.

One morning, Hassan's father burst through the door and jumped up and down. "We're in! We're in!" His mother ran from the kitchen cheering. So did Auntie Mona and Uncle Mazen.

"In where?" Hassan asked.

They all started dancing and singing in the tiny living room, too happy to answer. Hassan grew impatient. "In *where*?" he shouted again.

Finally, Hassan's father pulled Hassan onto his lap and explained. "We're going to America! This is a very special moment in your life, Hassan. America is where dreams come true. Remember how I told you the Syrians were protesting because they dreamed of having freedom? In America, everyone has freedom."

America?

Hassan had seen countless shows about America. *Sesame Street. Power Rangers. Charlie and the Chocolate Factory.* That was America!

But he was nervous.

"What if none of the kids in America like me?" Hassan asked his father.

"Give them time, Hassan, and they will discover what a kind boy you are."

The paperwork at the airport read "Refugees" in large print on every page. Hassan had never heard that word before.

His father explained. "Refugees are people who have to leave one home in search of another. So many people in Syria have become refugees, Hassan. I want you and Lina to have a bright future. So we will make America our new home. And you will have a beautiful future, God willing."

Hassan got to ride on an airplane to America. They flew higher than the birds and the buildings, and even the clouds.

With his face pressed against the oval-shaped window, he remembered his friends from home, especially Samir and Omar. He wondered if he would ever see them again. He wondered if they made new friends, or if he would make friends in America who were as fun and as nice as they were.

As he remembered all the places his family had been, all the things they had seen since leaving Syria, he drifted off to sleep, his arms wrapped around his soccer ball, the one piece of home he had left.

After a long and tiring flight, they
landed in a city called Denver. A woman
with golden hair and a big smile
welcomed his family to America. Her
name was Sandy. A man named Ismail was with her. He also
came from Syria and gave Hassan a high five when they met.

"You like soccer, I see," Ismail said to Hassan. "There are lots of places where you can play here."

Sandy and Ismail took Hassan and his family to a small apartment building, where a lot of people spoke different languages. The apartment was small, just like Uncle Mazen's apartment in Austria.

Hassan's father thanked Sandy and Ismail, and closed the door. He turned to look at his family. "Welcome home," he said.

It took about two months, but the day finally came when Hassan was ready to start school. He had studied English since arriving in America because his parents said they don't speak Arabic at the school he was going to.

When it came time for recess, Hassan went to his school bag and took out his soccer ball. He always kicked it around during recess back in Syria. When he got outside, all the kids were playing with each other. None played with him. He kicked his ball against the school's brick walls. Suddenly, a bigger kid came over to him, pushed him to the ground, and laughed.

"Why did you do that?" Hassan shouted. But the boy just pointed and laughed at him.

"You talk funny," the bully said, making the other boys laugh again. "You look funny too!"

Hassan fought back tears. He didn't want the bully to see him cry. He wished his family never left Syria.

Just then, a different group of boys came over and shouted at the bully, "Get out of here! Get out of here, or we'll tell on you!"

The bully and his friends saw they were outnumbered and walked away.

One boy walked over to Hassan, smiled, and held out his hand to help him up. Hassan hesitated at first, but then he let the boy help him.

"I'm Michael. What's your name?" the boy asked. He had red hair, freckles, and a missing tooth right up front.

"I am Hassan."

Just then, three of Michael's friends walked over. One of them was carrying Hassan's soccer ball. "Is this your ball?" a boy named Lucas asked. "Do you want to play?"

Hassan nodded, a smile gradually growing on his face.

Michael liked to bounce the ball off his head and knees. And he was really good at it.

Lucas was a tall, skinny, African American boy. He was really fast. Maybe even faster than Hassan's friend Omar!

There was Prashant, whose family moved to Denver from India a few years earlier. He liked to play goalie and teased all the boys trying to get the ball past him.

Then there was Jose. His family came from Mexico, the country next to America. He was very funny, always telling jokes and doing funny dances whenever he scored a goal.

They all looked so different from each other. But in a lot of ways, they had so much in common.

It wasn't long before Hassan was darting up and down the field at school, laughing and having a great time with his new friends. It felt just like home.

About the Author

Vivian Salama covers the White House for the Wall Street Journal. She previously worked as a foreign correspondent for over a decade, reporting from more than sixty countries. Salama served as the AP's bureau chief in Iraq from 2014-2016.

Printed in the United States
By Bookmasters